*Growing up in*
# HINDUISM

## Jacqueline Hirst with Geeta Pandey

Series editor: Jean Holm

D1314778

## What is this book about?

One of the most interesting ways to learn about a religion is to try to see it through the eyes of children who are growing up in a religious family. In this way we can discover something of what it *feels* like to belong to the religion.

In the books in this series we shall be finding out how children gradually come to understand the real meaning of the festivals they celebrate, the scriptures and other stories they hear, the ceremonies they take part in, the symbols of their religion and the customs and traditions of their religious community. This should provide a good foundation for going on to a wider study of the religions.

The five books in this series deal with the main religions that are found in Britain today: Christianity, Hinduism, Islam, Judaism and Sikhism. However, some things are more important in one religion than in another. For example, festivals play a bigger part in the lives of Jewish children than they do in the lives of Sikh children, and the scriptures play a bigger part in the lives of Muslim children than they do in the lives of Hindu children, so although many of the same topics are dealt with in all the books, the pattern of each book is slightly different.

There are differences within every religion as well as between religions, and even a very long book could not describe the customs and beliefs of all the groups that make up a religion. In these books we may be learning more about one of the groups, or traditions, within the religion, but there will be references to the different ways in which other groups practise their faith.

In this series of books we are using BCE (Before the Christian Era) and CE (in the Christian Era) instead of BC and AD, which refer to Christian beliefs about the significance of Jesus.

## How to use this book

Some of you will be studying religions for the first time. Others may already have learnt something about places of worship or festivals, and you will be able to gain greater understanding and fit what you know into a wider picture of the religion.

As you learn about how children grow up in a religion, prepare a display, or perhaps make a large class book. You will find some suggestions of activities in the text, but you will be able to think of many more. If your display is good enough it might be possible to put it up in the hall or in a corridor so that lots of people can see it. Try to show what it feels like to be on the 'inside' of the religion, so that other pupils and teachers and visitors to the school will be able to learn about the religion from the point of view of the children who are growing up in it.

# Contents

# Worship

## Learning the patterns of Hinduism

On the mantelpiece in the Pandeys' front room gleams a brass lamp. Its stand is in the shape of the Om. It is one of the many objects with which Shivani has grown up.

### "Om namaha Ganeshāya"

The Om sound is a very ancient Hindu symbol. The wise say it can lead to the highest truth (**Brahman**)*. Yet children can use it in their prayers. Gradually they may learn to understand its 'hundreds of meanings' more deeply. The same happens with festivals and celebrations. As children join in and watch others at worship, they learn the patterns of their religion and start to see what they may mean.

Hinduism is a vast religion which embraces many different traditions and customs. It comes from the great land of India, with its varied languages, regions and ways of life. In this book, Hindus living in the UK talk about growing up in different ways, in India, East Africa and Britain. They describe worship, festivals and rites and relationships, to help others share some of the experiences of growing up in Hinduism.

* The words in the glossary are printed in **bold** type the first time they appear in the book. A pronunciation guide is given with the glossary and index (→ pages 62−63).

4

*"The Om sound is very important. We start all our prayers with it. I have been told it has hundreds of meanings, but one is that you are saying 'Welcome' to God."*

Look at the photograph of the front room of a Hindu home in England. A small image of Shiva sits on a shelf. In the centre of the shelf is a photograph of the grandparents, and to the left of that is a photograph of the Shivling from the Vishvanath Temple at Varanasi in India. A brass lamp in the shape of the Om is on the lower shelf. Among the family books may be a copy of the *Bhagavata Purana* in **Sanskrit** or perhaps the *Ramayan* in Hindi. Upstairs in the parents' room is a shrine where the gods are worshipped every day.

*The front room of a Hindu home in England.*

# Recognising forms of God

Pictures of the gods and goddesses may be all around a Hindu home. Devotional pictures may be seen on calendars as well as in the shrine. To Hindu children, as to others, their many forms are the source of constant questions:

Why does Lakshmi have four arms?
Why does Ganesh have an elephant head?
Why are there so many gods?
Whom do we worship?

**One God really**

*"There is only one God really, who takes many different forms. The main forms are Shiva and Vishnu. Vishnu is worshipped as Rama and Krishna. Then there is the Goddess. She too has many forms — Lakshmi, Parvati, Durga, Ambaji, Kali. We have a picture of Durga in our* **puja** *room."*

**Why are there so many gods?**

*"The gods took different forms according to the time and the job which had to be done. Vishnu and Lakshmi became Ram and Sita, because Ravan was terrorising the world. And Hanuman took his special monkey form, because he was going to serve Sri Ram."*

Rama.

Durga.

Lakshmi.

6

*Vishnu.*

*Shiva.*

*Chosen forms*

Although they may believe there is really only one God, most Hindus have a chosen form (**ishtadeva**), whom they prefer to worship. Often a god is worshipped because the person has felt that god's blessing in the past, perhaps at a time of illness or anxiety. Both these girls follow their mothers, who worship Shiv and Durga respectively:

*"I think my favourite god is Shiv. He seems powerful in the stories and kind at the same time. All the gods are like that, but he is the best."*

*"My friend in London, Jyoti, her favourite is the goddess, Durga. Durga is brave and kind. I don't know whether Jyoti is brave, but she is very kind, like Durga."*

---

*Spelling of names*

You will notice in this book that there are different spellings for the same name: Shiva/Shiv, Rāma/Rām, Rāmáyana/ Rāmáyan.

'Shiva' is the way this name is pronounced in Sanskrit, the language of the ancient Hindu scriptures. 'Shiv' is the way the name is pronounced in many modern Indian languages. The modern form has been kept in the quotations, but the Sanskrit version has been used in explanations.

# How can the gods be seen?

Here is a description of a young Hindu girl at the Cultural Festival of India. She is standing by the temple of Radha and Krishna.

## The image of Radha

The little girl's face lit up as she gazed at the image of Radha.
"Isn't she beautiful?" she sighed.

She wasn't just seeing a statue with gold jewellery and a rich red sari. She was seeing the goddess herself — there in the **murti** of Radha.

Then she turned quickly and started telling stories of Radha's flute-playing companion, Krishna. Stories of his childhood pranks, when he stole his mother's butter. Tales of his love for the cowherd girls who were enchanted by his silver-tongued flute.

She was learning of God's love for his worshippers, as she repeated the stories she'd heard. And she was seeing God in those images — taking **darshan**, as it is called.

'Darshan' means 'sight'. The gods can appear to humans in many different ways. Through their images or pictures, the gods grant darshan to their worshippers. This was what the little girl was experiencing as she stood before the image of Radha.

*"The gods have these images or forms. They're not really like that, but they help us to imagine and understand. Lakshmi has four arms to show she is very powerful. The ten heads of the demon king, Ravan, show that he had the intelligence of many human minds. Krishna plays the flute to call his worshippers to him. It's just the same with the stories."*

> As you go through the book, build up a list of the different gods and goddesses. Make a note of features which will help you to recognise them. Write down what they are holding, whom they are with, what colour their skin is and so on. For example, Krishna is shown as blue, often holds a flute and has a peacock feather in his headdress.

*Murtis of Radha and Krishna in a temple set up at Alexandra Palace, London, for the Cultural Festival of India, in 1985.*

# Stories of the gods

There are hundreds of well-known stories about different gods and goddesses.

Although some adults study the *Bhagavadgita* or even the *Upanishads*, these holy books are very difficult to understand. The stories told to children are more likely to come from the *Puranas* or from the world-famous *Ramayana*. From a very early age, children delight in their favourites.

*"I can remember when we were little, I loved to hear the stories. My father would tell them to my brother and me just at bedtime. We would imagine the gods. Then when we saw them in pictures and images, we could remember the stories.*

*If I had children, I'd tell them stories from the Ramayan. They are really about what people are like — cunning and sly, or good and kind — and what life is like, how people behave. But Ram was really God. So he shows us what we should be like."*

## The story of Rama and Sita

Banished to the forest for fourteen years, Prince Rama lives with his beautiful wife, Sita, and loyal half-brother, Lakshmana. One day, the brothers go into the forest in pursuit of a golden deer. Seeing a holy man, Sita goes to fulfil her duty and offers him rice. At once, Ravana, the ten-headed demon, reveals his true identity and kidnaps her. Finding her gone, the brothers embark on a long search. They are aided by the forest animals, in particular the monkeys and their faithful leader, Hanuman.

Hanuman leaps across the sea to find Sita imprisoned on the island of Lanka. True to Rama throughout her ordeal, Sita joyfully receives Rama's ring from the messenger. In the fighting which follows, Hanuman risks his life by setting fire to the city, using his own tail as a fire-brand. He returns to the Himalayas, uprooting a mountain to bring the herb which will cure the dying Lakshmana (→ pages 12−13).

At last, Ravana is slain by Rama, after a bitter battle. Rama and Sita return to rule their kingdom wisely, welcomed home with lights by their devoted subjects.

*"This one's excellent. You should read it."*

A popular way of telling the stories is in comic form. Shivani's recommendation is the story of how Parvati won Shiva's love by her penance and devotion. Their six-headed son, Karttikeya, saved the earth from great suffering, by killing the evil demon, Taraka.

The gods may also be presented on video. Watch Ram slay Ravan and rescue the beautiful Sita. Or learn of Santoshima's kindness to those who are devoted to her.

When people grow up in a religion like Hinduism, they gradually learn how stories, pictures, prayers and celebrations are linked with one another. They begin to see how these things affect the way people live their lives. For example, they might follow Hanuman's loyal devotion to God (Sri Ram).

Choose one form of God mentioned in this book, say Shiva or Lakshmi or Hanuman. To help other people understand it, present pictures and stories and prayers on your chosen form. Try to explain their special meanings and suggest how these stories and prayers might give an example to follow in life.

# Prayers and stories

It is not just stories which children are taught when young. Many prayers said by adult Hindus were learnt when they were children. Perhaps they were taught a prayer to help them at a particular time and that prayer has remained special for them ever since. Geeta explains how she learnt the prayer below.

*"Soon after my father died, I started having nightmares. I thought I could hear him calling me or see him standing near my bed.*

*My mother was very worried. In the end, she asked me to say the 'Hanuman Chalisa' prayer every night before I went to bed. This I did. The idea was to take my mind off what was worrying me.*

*After a couple of weeks, I felt much better. The prayer helped me to fight fear. It also gave me confidence, so I could carry out my family duties when we were going through a difficult time."*

## Hanuman Chalisa

O Lord Hanuman, you are an ocean of knowledge,
You can enlighten heaven and earth,
You are the son of Anjani and have great courage.
You have earrings in your ears, lovely hair, the sacred thread on your shoulder,
a mountain on your left hand, a huge weapon on your right.
You have helped Ram by burning Lanka,
bringing a message from Sita, killing all the demons.
You have pleased Ram by bringing life-saving herbs for Lakshman.
Vibhishan became the king of Lanka with your help.
You crossed the vast ocean, keeping Ram's ring in your mouth and met Sita in Lanka.
A person who will pray to you every day will never be frightened, but will be able to overcome diseases and depression in life.

The story of Rama and Sita, told in the *Ramayana*, is one of the best known of all Hindu stories (→ page 10). It has been told in many languages. This Hindi prayer recalls many of the events in the story where Hanuman showed great courage.

People pray to Hanuman hoping that he will give courage to them and take away all fears and problems.

*Lord Hanuman, the monkey god and faithful servant of Lord Ram.*

# Chants and songs

Hindu children hear many chants and prayers, but some are specially taught to them. The **Gayatri Mantra** is a good example of this. Traditionally, it is said by **brahmins** as part of their morning worship.

*The Gayatri Mantra written in Sanskrit. The words below are a transliteration of the Gayatri Mantra. The Sanskrit words are written in the letters used for English to show how to pronounce them. The English translation is below the prayer.*

   Om bhur bhuvah svahah
tat savitur varenyam
   bhargo devasya dhimahi
dhiyo yo nah pracodayat.

Let us meditate on the excellent splendour of the sun-god, Savitri. May he stir our thoughts.

*"Chanting steadies the mind. My mother taught me. Even my five year old nephew can chant. Before he goes to bed, he chants the Gayatri Mantra five times. It's in Sanskrit, so it's very difficult. Some people say the chants in English now, but they sound so long and dreary."*

---

Write out the Gayatri Mantra in Sanskrit.
Then try to learn one of the prayers on pages 14–15, by repeating it over and over.

*"The other day we had a concert in our house. The singer came from Bombay. She opened her beautiful programme with a Sanskrit hymn to Lord Ganesh. The words say that there is only one God, who is beyond all human thoughts. The children did not understand this, but they did recognise the name of Ganesh. They know that all new events start with a prayer to the god who removes obstacles."*

Unborn, beyond shape and form, the One,
Full bliss of the absolute, beyond bliss,
Supreme, from qualities and desires free,
O Ganesh, Supreme Reality, may I worship you.

Later in the concert, the singer sang **bhajans** to Lord Krishna. Some of the audience thought back to their childhood in India, when fifty or sixty people would gather to praise Krishna in song. Through such **satsangs** in this country too, songs can be handed down. Children can absorb the atmosphere of the singers' devotion to God.

| | |
|---|---|
| Jaya Ganesh jaya Ganesh | Hail Ganesh, hail Ganesh, |
| Jaya Ganesh deva | Hail Lord Ganesh, |
| mata teri Parvati | Your mother is Parvati, |
| pita Mahadeva. | Your father is Mahadeva (Shiva). |

*"This is a Hindi prayer we say to Ganesh every evening. I heard my mum saying it and now I can join in too."*

# Worshipping at home

Prayers may be said at any time. But many Hindus, particularly women, try to keep a special time each day for doing puja at the home shrine.

*Puja*

*"Puja is the offering of prayers to God every day. In India, we do this in the morning, but here life is so busy. In the evening, I have my shower and change my clothes. Then I go straight to the little room which is my temple. I do **arti** every evening and say a couple of lines from the Hanuman Chalisa. Shivani joins me some days, but if it is a festival I make sure she worships with me.*

*A woman is not allowed to do puja during menstruation. Shivani will do puja for me then. Our belief is that we must be pure for God.*

*Before you do puja, you can light some incense sticks and lamps to decorate the shrine. There is a lovely aroma from them. When you decorate the murtis with flowers, it makes you feel beautiful too.*

*You start by taking a little water. With some cotton wool, you wipe the pictures of the gods, as if you're imagining you're giving them a bath. Then you take a little red powder and make a paste with water. With the fourth finger of your right hand, you put a mark on the forehead of the god in each picture.*

*Next, you offer sweets or fruit to the gods.*

*Lastly, we do arti. A lamp is gently moved clockwise in front of the gods. While we do this, we say the arti prayers. My prayer is to Shiv. It is like saying to the gods, 'Now we have fed and decorated you, you can rest'. It shows how much we care for our gods.*

*When you have finished arti, you must take arti. So must anyone else who is in the house. You place your hands above the lamp flame with your finger-tips touching. Then you move your hands over your forehead to show you are receiving the blessing of God.*

*You must have **prashad** too. It doesn't matter if you have a hundred **ladoos** or just one. A single piece must be given to everyone who is present. It is like the food that God has left over. Of course, he can't eat really, but the idea is that we should eat it as a blessing from God."*

*"If we take off our shoes, we are allowed to go into our parents' room and do arti at the shrine to our gods. My two and a half year old nephew comes in and says,* **'Jay jay,'** *while his grandmother does her puja. This is how I shall teach my children."*

As these accounts show, children learn to do puja by watching their mothers, joining in and sometimes making the offerings themselves. As well as learning what to do, they will probably pick up the lovely atmosphere of arti. In this way, they may come to realise how important it is to be pure for God, in body and in mind; and how honoured a person is to receive God's blessing.

*In Hindu homes, there will be a shrine, a place where the gods are worshipped. It may be on a shelf or a small cupboard. Sometimes a whole room is made into a private temple. The shrine in this photograph is very elaborate because it has been prepared for the Divali festival.*

# Going to the temple

For Hindus, the home is very important as a place of worship. You can be extremely religious and hardly ever visit a temple. In Britain, you may live in a town which has no Hindu temple or where the Indian language spoken is not one you know well (→ page 23). Or your particular group may prefer to gather in members' homes. Even so, for many people, temples do play a major part in their growing up as Hindus.

*"I like going to the Southall temple, because the one we have in the house is not very large. I feel it's a bit more official. You can actually put a garland round the necks of the murtis and give money. The murtis seem more like God. It's so peaceful. You can just sit and say your prayers in silence. Here, at home there's always a lot going on. There, you can just concentrate and talk to him."*

*"When we lived in Mombasa (Kenya), there were four temples. We used to go to one each day, especially during Shravan (July—August). Arti was held every morning and evening. The morning one was too early, 6 a.m., so we went in the evening to receive prashad. In the month of Shravan, there would also be a programme of bhajans and readings from the scriptures."*

*"In South India, the morning arti could be very early, say, 4 or 5 o'clock. It was wonderful when we were there. All the bells were ringing and you could hear the chanting of* **mantras.** *It made you feel very purified."*

*The picture opposite shows a gopuram. These towering gateways form entrances to South Indian temple courtyards. They are highly decorated with sculptures of gods, humans and animals. The idea is to leave behind this busy world as you go through the gateway to approach the inner shrine and seek the truth within you.*

# Worshipping in the temple

*Temples may contain several different shrines. The main shrine in this temple is to Radha and Krishna. It also has shrines to Rama and Sita, to Shiva and to Ambaji, besides several others.*

Worship in the temple is similar to worship at home. In the temple, though, it is the priest who does the puja. He bathes the gods, decorates them with garlands, offers them food and performs the arti ceremony.

People come into the temple to worship individually. A father gives his son a coin to drop into the box at Sri Ram's shrine. Together, they take darshan, looking at the murtis and realising God's presence. After walking round the shrine clockwise, they take arti from the **diva** burning there. Perhaps some men will be chanting and the child will recognise the Hanuman Chalisa.

During congregations for the daily arti services, young children usually stay with their mothers. As the priest goes from shrine to shrine, the women turn to face each shrine in turn, copied by their children. The melodies of the chants to each god soon become familiar and the children pick up the words as they are sung over and over again. Imitating the adults, they learn to take arti. Often they get the job of giving a piece of paper to each person. On this, the sweet prashad is placed, when it is distributed at the end of the service.

*This is a simplified version of one of the most well-known melodies for the arti chant, 'Om jay jagdish hare'. The words vary, depending on which god the chant is addressing.*

21

# Temple activities

Temples are not just places where individuals may go and worship. At festival times, they will be packed out with huge crowds. Outside India, they are often community centres as well.

*"Last summer, there was a six day festival to raise money for a new temple in Harrow. Every day about 5,000 people came. The organisers set up a huge marquee and made an agreement with the police about parking.*

*A young professor from India was reading the* Bhagavata Purana *with its stories about Lord Krishna. After each little bit in Sanskrit, he would explain its meaning in Hindi and Gujarati. Then he would go over it in English, because some of the children there didn't even understand Gujarati.*

*We enjoyed it so much we bought a copy of the video. It's really an explanation of what life is like. The speaker made lots of jokes and gave everyday examples, so even the children could understand it."*

In India, public readings from the great holy books are common. Visiting **swamis** from India carry on the tradition in Britain and are treated with great respect. A special couch in the temple may be kept for such speakers and for reading the scriptures. On such occasions, children see how the swamis are looked up to for their knowledge of the scriptures. It gives them an opportunity to learn the age-old stories in a serious yet lively way.

The temple may also run regular classes for children. Some are to teach children to read and write their family's Indian language: Gujarati, Punjabi, Bengali or Hindi, for example. Others are more like Sunday schools. They help children to understand their religion and explain it to others. These classes are often set up by modern Hindu groups like the **Swaminarayan Movement** or **ISKCON**, which publishes beautifully illustrated story books for children in English.

*"I can speak Gujarati but I can't read it. After we came here from Uganda, there were no classes here."*

*"Every Saturday morning and one evening a week, we go to Gujarati classes. It's very hard work. The letters in Gujarati are very difficult to make, but I am learning so I can read the stories and prayers."*

*"We have always talked to our daughter in Hindi and in English, so she can understand both languages. She listens to me saying the arti prayers in Hindi and in Sanskrit and joins in. I don't think she could understand her religion properly if she just spoke English."*

*Part of a Hindi alphabet chart.*

---

*Indian languages*

There are fourteen major languages spoken in India today (including English). Most have their own alphabet or script. The North Indian languages, like Hindi, Punjabi, Gujarati and Bengali, have developed from Sanskrit ($\longrightarrow$ page 7) – a bit like Italian and French coming from Latin. The South Indian languages, like Tamil and Kannada, form a different family. Many Hindus living in Britain can speak at least two languages and understand a third or fourth.

Here is 'Happy Divali' written in Hindi, Gujarati and Tamil:

शुभ दीपावली
Hindi

શુભ દીવાલી
Gujarati

தீபாவளி வாழ்த்துகள்
Tamil

# Times and seasons

## A festival feeling

It is not just in day-to-day life that home and temple have parts to play for children growing up as Hindus. At festival time, home and temple have their own atmospheres of excitement and celebration.

At home, a special bath may be taken and new clothes worn. Particular care is taken with the puja. Often a sort of fast is carried out and vegetarian food is eaten. There are delicious sweets and visitors all the time.

In the temple, crowds throng, calm yet expectant. Chattering families greet relatives and friends. Outsiders are welcomed. There is an air of anticipation — a festival feeling.

*A crowded temple at festival time.*

# When to celebrate

*"When does Navratri start this year, Mum?"*
*"I'm not sure. Go and check the pattra."*

So that they know exactly when to celebrate, most Hindus have a pattra or special calendar. This matches up the months of the Hindu year with the months in a January to December calendar. It is needed because most Hindu calendars are based on the moon, rather than the sun. Each Hindu month has a 'light fortnight', which leads up to the full moon, and a 'dark fortnight', which ends with the new moon.

*Pattra*

*"We usually get our pattra from India. If someone is coming, I ask them to bring one for me. This year, we got ours from Southall in London. Gujaratis have different charts from us, so they'll get theirs from somewhere else, Leicester maybe, or their part of London."*

The Hindu year varies from region to region in India. For example, some Hindus have New Year in Chaitra (called 'Chittrai' in Tamil), others at the beginning of Karttika. Children get used to consulting the family pattra and seeing when in the dark or light fortnights particular festivals fall. They also learn from the pattra which are the good times for ceremonies like the baby's first haircut (→ page 55).

| Here is a chart of the months in Hindi: | | | | | |
| --- | --- | --- | --- | --- | --- |
| HINDI MONTHS | INTERNATIONAL CALENDAR | FESTIVALS | HINDI MONTHS | INTERNATIONAL CALENDAR | FESTIVALS |
| Chaitra | March/April | | Ashvin | Sept/Oct | |
| Vaishakh | April/May | | Karttik | Oct/Nov | |
| Jyesth | May/June | | Agrahayan | Nov/Dec | |
| Ashadh | June/July | | Paush | Dec/Jan | |
| Shravan | July/August | | Magh | Jan/Feb | |
| Bhadrapad | August/Sept | | Phalgun | Feb/March | |

Draw the chart above. Then find out when the festivals mentioned in this book are celebrated, so you can fill them in in the extra column of your chart.

# Favourite festivals

There are probably more festivals in Hinduism than in any other religion. But for most families, some festivals will be more important than others.

*"My favourite festival is Divali because of the fireworks and things. We have sparklers and we make lots of sweets. I like* **burfi** *the best, the kind covered in silver. I've helped roll out the* **gulab jamon** *since I was about six. We had loads of people come from India that Divali. It was excellent."*

*"All the festivals are important. You can't really choose between them. If I had to, I'd say Divali and Holi, because most Hindus celebrate these two in this country. And for me, Shivratri, because Shiv is my special god. And Rakshabandhan. This is very important for brahmins like us."*

*"The main festival for us is Navratri. We Gujaratis do have big celebrations for Divali, but the dancing at Navratri is really the best. The festival goes on for nine nights and the hall is always packed."*

*"If you go to the temple next Sunday night, that is the most important time in our year. At midnight, Lord Krishna is born."*

These people give lots of reasons for a festival's importance: their home region in India, caste, chosen god and sheer enjoyment! Whichever festivals are most important in their family, Hindu children are involved. As they help with preparations and listen to the stories, they become part of the pattern of celebration which goes on from year to year.

---

To help other people understand that pattern, use this section of the book to build up material for:

a chart of Hindu festivals throughout the year (⟶ page 25);
a collection of festival stories;
a taste of festival cookery;
a display of festival patterns;
a sense of 'festival feeling' as part of growing up in Hinduism.

---

It would be impossible to describe even a few festivals in detail here. Instead, this section will try to show why festivals are such special times in the lives of Hindu children.

*Festivals and fasting*

One way in which the Hindu year is shaped is by times of fasting and celebration (→ page 25). Some religions make a great difference between fasting and feasting. For Hindus, fasts and festivals often go together. At some festivals, a fast may lead up to a feast. At others, some foods may be avoided, while others are enjoyed. Children soon get to know which treats come when!

*"On special days we fast. There are different kinds of fasts. On the birthdays of the gods — Shivratri, Ramnavami and Krishnajanmashtami — we don't take any cereals or meats or eggs. The idea is to make the day different. We give up ordinary foods and eat special things instead. It shows we will go to trouble for our gods as well as enjoying ourselves."*

*Rasgulla (centre front) and jalebi, sweets in sticky syrup, which are popular with children at festival time.*

## Ramnavami

*(ninth day of light half of Chaitra)*

Rama's birthday is one of these special days of fasting. Sometimes the stories of Rama's life are read in the temple, during the days leading up to the festival. Hanuman, Rama's faithful servant, has a special place. Puja is done with great care.

*"On this day and on Shivratri, I wipe the god's face with Gangajal. This is water from the River Ganges. In this country, I only have a small bottle, so I just use it on special occasions. Some people may think this is silly, but it's my way of showing devotion to God. My daughter watches me doing this. She knows it is one of the days when we don't eat meat or cereals to keep ourselves pure for God."*

# Krishnajanmashtami

*(eighth day of the dark half of Shravan at midnight)*

Lord Krishna's birthday is also marked by fasting and readings from the scriptures. Decorating the shrines and waiting for midnight help children to share the great sense of anticipation, as Krishna's birth draws near.

*"When we lived in India, the preparations started days beforehand. We would give money for decorating the temple, maybe up to a thousand* **rupees.** *And we had a special corner in our house with lights, glitter, tinsel and fresh leaves. We put toys here — and little models of Krishna crossing the river, killing the snake-demon Kaliya, holding up Mount Govardhan to shelter the cowherds — all stories from Lord Krishna's life.*

*We would fast up till midnight. Thirty or forty ladies would come to our house and we would have* **kirtan** *till 12 o'clock. Then just at midnight, we would have a big puja and arti to celebrate Lord Krishna's birth. Afterwards, we shared prashad. We had a delicious milk drink with yoghurt, honey, sugar and Gangajal in. We drank it out of little clay cups which you threw away afterwards. I still make charnamrit, the milk drink, on Janmashtami — but not with Gangajal in England. My daughter loves it."*

*Sweets offered to Krishna.*

*Krishna's cradle placed in front of curtains.*

## A cradle for Krishna

*"We always have a cradle for Janmashtami. At midnight, everyone takes one of the cords attached to the cradle to rock the baby Krishna. It's a lovely time for children."*

In the temple, curtains are closed in front of the Radhakrishna shrine till midnight. Gifts have been brought and placed near Krishna's cradle. After midnight, mothers bring their children to look at the baby Krishna.

At midnight, the curtains of the shrine are drawn back. Radha and Krishna are revealed in all their festival glory. At their feet lie sweets and other offerings in abundance.

Find out in which ways celebrations of Krishna's birthay and Jesus' are similar. How are they different? Try to suggest reasons for these differences.

# Rakshabandhan

The festival of Rakshabandhan falls on the full moon of Shravan, just before Krishna's birthday. Originally a brahmin festival, it is now celebrated by most Hindus. Children join in with the thread-tying.

*Knots of protection*

The name means 'a tie of protection'. It refers to the main custom which is practised at home rather than in the temple. Sisters tie a thread or tinsel bracelet to their brother's wrist.

As the girl ties the rakhi, she says these words: "May his ambitions be fulfilled in life." In turn, her brother gives her a present and promises to protect her all through life.

*"I don't have a brother so I tied a rakhi to my cousin's wrist. It was his right wrist. It was like a flower with orange in the middle. It had some black in. There was a silver bit at the bottom and a pink spot right in the middle. He gave me a dress."*

*Rakhi tied to a boy's wrist.*

*Other knots*

Threads are also tied as a symbol of protection at other times in life. Some Gujaratis tie a black thread round the right wrist of a mother-to-be at the beginning of the fifth month of her first pregnancy. This is done by the father-to-be's sister and is meant to protect the baby.

Babies may have black threads tied round their wrists too. Again, it symbolises being kept safe from evil. Black is an inauspicious colour, so it's like hoping that bad luck will keep away.

Knots also play a part in the sacred thread ceremony and in weddings (⟶ pages 48, 52). In some traditions, not only is the bride's sari knotted to the cloth round the groom's neck, a braided cord is looped around their necks to symbolise the joining of bride and groom and their families.

*"I'd like to go to India. My red wedding sari is still tied to the white cloth which goes round us when we are being married. I can't wear my sari till the knot is undone. That has to be done by a priest in India. Some families untie the knot here. My brother and sister-in-law have done, because my family doesn't mind. But my husband and I have to do what my mother-in-law wishes, so we shall go to India. There are a lot of things we have to do when we untie the knot."*

The knot is a powerful symbol of being united and kept safe together. The great trouble which is taken over untying it is a warning about the dangers of broken relationships.

As they watch these different ceremonies and tie the threads themselves, children are not just learning about the visible knots. They are experiencing the strong bonds of affection which draw brothers and sisters together. They may feel a sense of community with others who have the same customs. And they begin to realise the importance of permanent relationships and vows.

# Navratri, Durgapuja and Dassehra

*(first—tenth days of light half of Ashvin)*

While Rakshabandhan is celebrated in much the same way throughout India, other festivals vary enormously from region to region.

All over India, after the monsoon, people hold a nine-night festival, with more festivities on the tenth day. But they don't all call it by the same name or celebrate in the same way.

Here is a description of Navratri ('Nine Nights') by a girl whose family comes from Gujarat, where she lived till she was twelve.

*Gujarati celebrations*

*"The thing I remember most about Navratri in India is the dancing. There was dancing every night. From about the age of seven, my sister would sit there with her hand on her chin, watching and counting. And then she knew how to join in herself.*

*I liked the stick dances best. We decorated our own* **dandyas**. *You can make them any colour, but it's nice if they're red and green.*

*Navratri's so colourful. We try not to wear black (→ page 30). On big festival days, we like to wear bright colours — red, green, yellow, orange. It makes you feel good."*

Navratri is a very important festival for Gujarati Hindus. In Britain, temples are often packed to overflowing. Sometimes, caste associations arrange their own celebrations, hiring large halls so everyone has a chance to join in the dancing.

Two dances are traditional: the garba (circle dance) and the dandya ras (stick dance). Prizes are often awarded for the best performances. The dancers are traditionally female, accompanied by women musicians playing and singing bhajans.

Some say the women are like the **gopis**, who danced with their beloved Krishna all night. Others think of the Goddess, who is worshipped in her different forms each evening of Navratri.

*"The Goddess in her kind form is called Durga. Her energy survives in us all. But we have to wake up her energy in us, which we try to do in the dance."*

*Girls performing the stickdance.*

Durga's energy is famous from a story on which the Bengali celebrations of this festival are based. It is Durga's energy which destroys the evil buffalo demon, Mahisha, and rescues the earth which is suffering. Her energy can help people overcome evil in their own lives, so they can live in a pure and kind way — like Jyoti who worships Durga because she is very kind and brave (→ page 7).

The dances often take place round a madh. This is a moveable shrine which has pictures of different forms of the Goddess on each of its six faces. Sometimes young girls will be dressed up and honoured as if they were the Goddess herself.

## Bengali Durgapuja

Bengalis call the festival 'Durgapuja'. It is the most important time of year in Bengal, where worship of Durga is very popular. Like Navratri, Durgapuja lasts for nine nights, but the last three are the most important. The day after — the tenth of the fortnight — the festival images of Durga are thrown into the water. Children learn that it is not the images themselves which are worshipped, but the Goddess who is present in the image.

*"Now we live in England, we all go down to London for Durgapuja, so we can celebrate together. The children can get some idea of the excitement of the festival.*

*In Bengal, there's an amazing atmosphere at this time of year. Everyone's saving up for new clothes and buying presents for relatives. People give money to hospitals and orphanages. You can buy 'Puja Numbers' of children's comics with the story of Durga in. And we spend hours and hours making delicious sweets.*

*Everywhere, there are festival images of Durga, set up by different groups. The shops are all open late during the festival. Everyone goes to a puja if they can.*

*When it's all over, each Durga image is taken to the river. As it goes under the water, it's like all the evil is being carried away. But you feel sad to see her go! We spend the rest of the day visiting people, offering sweets and eating them!"*

*Durga puja celebrations. At the close of the festivities, the Durga image will be immersed in the water.*

34

*North Indian-style celebrations*

In North India, this time of year brings the Ram-Lila. Huge puppets of the characters from the Ramayana are made and scenes from the story are acted out. On the tenth day, called Dassehra, Ravana is burnt on an enormous bonfire. Fireworks help celebrate his defeat ($\longrightarrow$ page 10).

Children in Britain often put on shadow puppet plays telling this part of the story for Divali. Strictly speaking, though, Divali celebrates a later episode, when Rama and Sita return home.

*In June 1987, pupils from schools all over London were able to share in the spirit of Hindu celebrations. They put on a spectacular performance of the Ramayana story, complete with giant puppets and a 'monkey' army!*

## A common theme

Gujarati Navratri, Bengali Durgapuja, North Indian Dassehra — just a few of the many different ways of celebrating these festivals. Other stories are told as well.

At first, all the different ways of doing things may seem confusing. But to children growing up in a Hindu home, it's not really complicated at all. Their family will celebrate the festival in the same way each year. They will pick up the dances, look forward to the presents, learn to make the sweets which are traditional in their family. They will hear the stories familiar to their way of celebrating.

Perhaps, as they become older, they will learn about other ways and stories and see a common theme. For Durga's slaying of Mahisha and Rama's defeat of Ravana both show colourfully and dramatically that good can overcome evil.

# Festival designs

One custom shared by Hindus all over the world is making designs to welcome the gods at festival times.

*This photograph shows a young girl making a* **rangoli** *pattern, ready for Navratri. The platform is in front of a shrine to Ambaji. The goddess, Ambaji, is worshipped by Gujaratis and is very similar to Durga, but rides a tiger, not a lion.*

'Rangoli' is a Gujarati word. The Hindi word is 'chauk'. Bengalis say 'alpana'. It is traditional to make the patterns with rice-flour, but nowadays people use anything suitable, like chalk. There aren't any particular patterns, but fish and flower shapes are meant to be lucky.

Rangoli design competitions are especially popular at Divali time. Children learn by watching others at work.

*Child's rangoli design.*

*"You make these patterns for any festival. It's like welcoming God into your house, by putting down a red carpet. The idea is, you can't put God on a bare floor.*

*For Divali, I will make a rangoli on the kitchen table, because I shall say a special puja in the kitchen. I also do this for Karvachauth. This is a fast which comes just before Divali. It's for the welfare of your husband."*

*"This year, I helped make the patterns for Karvachauth. I notice how Mum does it. Some people don't bother, but I look and see what she does. First, we make a moon, using white flour. We made a circle, then I put on the points. Not a special number. Just so it looks nice.*

*At Janmashtami, we were in India. My grandmother made the patterns for the worship herself, so they were exactly right."*

*Rangoli patterns for Shiva, Lord of the dance, at a performance of South Indian dancing.*

# Divali

*(thirteenth day of dark half of Ashvin to second day of light half of Karttik)*

The Hindu festival best known outside India is probably Divali. It is also a firm favourite with children.

There are many stories linked with the different days of the festival. Tales of Krishna's defeat of the demon Naraka, and King Bali's generosity, are at least as popular as the well-known story of the homecoming of Rama and Sita.

*Lighting the way*

In North India, the first of Karttik is New Year, so it is a time of new beginnings and hope. The previous day is the new moon day. Lakshmi, the goddess of prosperity, is worshipped for good fortune in the coming year. Her way is lit by millions of lamps and fairy lights. Their blaze of light on the darkest night of the year symbolises the victory of knowledge over ignorance, of goodness over evil. And it's the lights and the fireworks which, for many Hindu children, make this their favourite festival.

*"I can remember the fireworks in Mombasa. All the houses had verandahs and flat roofs where people slept in the summer. At Divali time, we'd wake up at 4 in the morning and let the fireworks off. Nobody minded, even though we had rockets that exploded!"*

Now in her twenties, her face lit up as she remembered the excitement and community spirit of Divali in Kenya. The same enthusiasm seems to be shared by Hindu children all over the world.

*"At school, we all made clay lamps and my mother came in to show the class how to make rangoli patterns. She wore a purple and gold sari and lots of gold jewellery, like we do for festivals.*

*In the evening, we had our celebrations in a hall in Cambridge. Everyone wore the new clothes they got for Divali. We had some dancing and a group of us did a shadow puppet play. There was a rangoli competition too. I drew lotus flowers in mine, because they're Lakshmi's favourite flower.*

*The fireworks were really lovely — Golden Fountains, Catherine Wheels, rockets — but it was ever so cold outside. Then they gave out* the prizes for the Ras and Garba from Navratri and we all had some Indian food to eat."

"In India, we children used to go round in a crowd. We would carry a diva in a clay pot, which had holes to let the light shine through. We'd sing songs — a bit like carol-singing. Then people would either give us money or **ghee** to keep our lamp burning. It was a good feeling, all going round in a group. Some people even put lamps on the rivers. They looked lovely floating there, till they were taken away by the deep waters."

*A young woman in northern India lights the Divali festival lamps.*

# Annakuth

*"Annakuth is our New Year. There are piles of sweets and savouries and drinks. We all go visiting one another and eat far too much! Some people spend the day in the temple. If you go to Neasden, there are 108 varieties of foods —* **jalebi,** *gulab jamon, burfi... A lot of care is taken because the food is offered to the gods."*

*The temple in Neasden during Annakuth.*

### Annakuth in London

In the space of an hour and a half, three lots of visitors called, children in tow. Tea and cold drinks were offered. Milk sweets were served. On a side table was a plate with dried grapes, sugar crystals and cinnamon.

News was exchanged and plans for the evening discussed. In the hall, a clay lamp was burning. Upstairs, two postcards and a picture of Lakshmi with Sarasvati and Ganesh had been added to the shrine for Lakshmipuja the day before.

We arrived at the temple in Neasden in time for the 3 o'clock arti. The sight was amazing — people everywhere, food banked high on a long stepped platform covered in an auspicious red cloth. A special **mandir** had been set up for Divali, with images of Ganesh, Rama and Sita, Lakshman, Hanuman and so on. As people filed past, parents encouraged their children to go right up to the mandir, reminding them of the characters and the part they played in the Ramayana story.

Although the temple is run by the Swaminarayan movement, there were lots of other Hindus there for the festival. All could join in with the arti chant which used a tune well-known in other Hindu temples. Children clapped in time; babies slept to its gentle sound. When the arti tray was brought round, children followed the adults in putting a coin on the plate and taking arti.

When the arti was over, there was a chance to file past the banks of food, enjoying the sight and smell of delicious sweets and pastries, which people had given. Later in the evening, it would be distributed to those still present. But there was still an opportunity to take prashad for those who left earlier. At the door, two men distributed bags of Bombay Mix to every single person who had come. If they were lucky, the children got two!

# Bhaibij

The day after New Year, brothers go to their married sisters and they will give them a special meal. The brothers will take a present for them in return. It's not really for children, but it does show how important family members are in an Indian family.

A Hindu girl said, "When I am married, my brother will come to me on Sisters' Day and I will cook him something which he really likes."

## Starting to choose

The girl who looked forward to being able to cook something special for her brother on Sisters' Day (→ page 41) was already starting to choose. She was saying that she would like to keep this Hindu family tradition in the future.

Like people in any religion, some Hindus will want to go on celebrating festivals just for the sake of tradition. Others, as they grow up, will see how festivals form part of a larger whole. Stories, worship, celebrations and relationships are seen as part of a pattern which acts as a guide for life.

Here is a glimpse of such a pattern as a mother and her young daughter describe the festival of Shivratri and say why it is important to them.

## Mahashivratri

*(fourteenth day of dark half of Magh)*

*"This is a very important festival for me because Shiv is my chosen god — the way I think about God for myself. In India, there's loads of fruit at this time of the year. We fast all day. We don't drink water either until midnight and we take offerings to the Shiv temple — milk, sandalwood paste, Gangajal, fruit. We must take the fruit of the bel tree and its leaves. Shiv is meant to have liked bel fruit and the leaves look like his trident. In the temple, people sing the Shiv Chalisa until midnight when Lord Shiv comes."* (Mother)

*"My favourite festival is Shivratri, because Shiv is my favourite god. I see Shiv as the most powerful god. When I look at the pictures, the snakes are always near him. I would never dare touch a poisonous snake, but the snake is actually fearing Shiv. It shows he has power over the whole world, not just humans. He can help us be brave and kind.*

*I think Shivratri must have been a wonderful day, such power being born. So that's why I would celebrate it. When I'm older, I would keep a fast through the day, if Shiv was my chosen god. I like the idea that you don't have to shave your hair off or anything like that to worship Shiv. You can just give what you have, even if it's only small.*

*There's a story about Shiv. There was this hunter and he was staying in this tree for the night. The leaves of the tree kept falling onto the ground. In the morning, the hunter saw there was a Shiv* **ling** *where the leaves had fallen."* (Daughter)

Hunters are regarded as sinful because they take life.
The story goes on to explain that Shiva received the leaves of the bel tree and the tears of the hunter as if they had been specially offered to him in worship. For Hindus this shows that Shiv accepts even sinful people.

Through worship at this festival and other times, children learn that God blesses his worshippers by accepting their offerings, however humble they are. Children may also be taught some words of Krishna about this, from the *Bhagavadgita*:

'Whoever offers to Me a leaf, a flower, a fruit or water with devotion, that offering of devotion, I will accept from the pure of heart.'

---

This verse (*Bhagavadgita* 9.26) is written below in Sanskrit. What does the verse suggest about what is important to Krishna — the size of the gift or the devotion with which it is given? What do you think matters most when you are giving something?

---

पत्रं पुष्पं फलं तोयं
यो मे भक्त्या प्रयच्छति ।
तदहं भक्त्युपहृत-
मश्नामि प्रयतात्मनः ॥ २६ ॥

# Playing Holi

*(Full moon of Phalgun)*

But life is not always serious. As the full moon approaches in February or March, preparations for the colourful festival of Holi will be under way. In India, children start stocking up with coloured powders. During Holi, they will squirt them with delight at one another and at unsuspecting passers-by. New clothes are bought and the delicacies of the region cooked.

Various stories are told at this time of year. In South India, people remember how Lord Shiva burnt to ashes Kama, the god of love, when he tried to interrupt Shiva's meditation. Around Mathura, where Lord Krishna spent his childhood, songs and dances recall the love of Krishna and the gopis. Perhaps the most famous story is about Prahlad, whose devotion to God could not be weakened.

Hiranyakashipu was a powerful king. He decided that people should worship him like God. But his son, Prahlad, a faithful worshipper of Lord Vishnu, refused to obey his father.

In the end, the king ordered his sister, Holika, to lure Prahlad into a roaring fire. Now Holika had been given a promise that she would never be burnt up. But Prahlad continued to pray to God and remained in the fire, while Holika, who had used her power selfishly, was consumed to ashes.

So, on Holi, bonfires may be lit and images of Holika or Kama burned. This symbolises getting rid of evil before the New Year, which, for many Hindus, starts two days later. Mothers will circle the bonfire, carrying children on their backs, and this prayer is often heard:

"May our children live a million years."

*Holi bonfire in Coventry.*

## Memories of Holi

"In India, we used to have different coloured powders — all colours, red, green, with glitter in. There was a big water-lily pond and we used to push people in. You get mad on that day!

We finished all that by about 2 o'clock. Then we had a bath. About 4 or 5 o'clock, all the children and adults put on new clothes. You wear lots of perfume and have clean hair. Then you go and see friends.

They offer you special sweets. At Holi, we always have gujhia, which we make at home. Wherever you go, you are offered a large glass of milkshake. It's made with yoghurt and cream, with nuts, sugar and vanilla in and it's absolutely delicious!"

"In this country, Holi's not like it's described, not in the traditional way. We just visit friends. The festival is for friendship really. All are together, no matter who they are, like the different colours mixing. Enemies should become friends, at least for that day."

|  | Gujhia |
|---|---|
| Pastry | 1 cup plain flour |
| | 4 tablespoons vegetable oil |
| | 3–4 tablespoons water |
| Filling | $\frac{1}{2}$ cup semolina |
| | $1\frac{1}{2}$ oz butter |
| | $\frac{1}{4}$ cup castor sugar |
| | $\frac{1}{2}$ tsp ground green cardamoms |
| | 10 almonds finely chopped |
| Method | Heat oil in deep frying pan on very low heat. |
| | Mix oil and flour by rubbing in. Add water gradually to make smooth dough (like flan pastry). |
| | Melt butter in shallow frying pan. Add semolina and fry on low heat till brownish. Keep stirring. Add sugar, ground cardamom and chopped almonds. Fry for two minutes until sugar mixes with semolina. Leave to cool. |
| | Break dough into small balls ($\frac{1}{2}$ size of ping pong ball). Roll each ball very thin to a 4 inch circle. Lift gently on flat of hand. Put 1 tbs of filling in middle. Brush and seal edges of pastry without pressing middle part. |
| | Fry a couple of gujhias at a time in oil until gently browned. |

# Rites and relationships

**"May our children live a million years."**

Of course, this Holi prayer is not meant to be taken literally. It is a prayer for the children's well-being. That desire for well-being is very important. It is at the heart of the various ceremonies or rites which take place at different stages in a person's life. It is also the concern of other members of a person's family and caste.

## Relationships

Lots of members of the family may have a hand in a child's upbringing. In India, it is often the grandparents who will tell the children stories and teach them about their religion. Aunts and uncles may also be on hand to spoil them. For when an older brother marries, he will often bring his wife to live in his parents' home.

In Britain, some Hindus choose to keep this pattern of living in an 'extended' family. Three generations may share a house or live very close together. Others prefer to live in a smaller family of just parents and children. Even so, they will probably keep close contact with other relatives, whether they live elsewhere in Britain or in India, eight thousand miles away.

### News of the family

"...I'm very busy at the moment. Both my sisters-in-law have just had babies. They're very sweet, but they do cry a lot. I look after my niece and nephew quite a bit. At least I shall know what to do when I'm older and have children of my own.

I enjoyed my visit to India, though wasn't it hot! We went to Kutch and Gujarat and we stayed in our village where my uncle has an ice cream shop. It was the first time I'd met my grandmother and my uncle's family and many other relatives. It's seven years since my father's been there. He was pleased to see his mother again, because she's getting quite old now. He said, 'God has been good to let me see her again'.

I hope you're both well and your father is feeling better..."

The letter on page 46 is from a teenager who lives with her parents and two sisters. Her two older brothers and their families live next door — plenty of baby-sitters on hand!

For Hindus, it is one of their five daily duties to show respect to their elders (⟶ page 56). Hindu children see the respect with which their parents treat their own parents (the children's grandparents). They understand that the same is expected of them — though this doesn't mean that they always agree with their parents!

As they become older, they may also realise how important a role grandparents can play, especially if they're not around.

*"Until my grandmother came over from India and stayed with us, I didn't really know how she did puja and that sort of thing. She did teach my mum when she was little, but she didn't try to force religion on her children. My mum's not really religious. We do keep festivals, but we don't do puja every day or anything like that.*

*But I would like to be able to teach my children, so they can choose for themselves. So I was glad when my grandmother came and I could learn from her."*

## Rites

Family members are always invited to come to special occasions in a person's life. These rites or **samskaras** are performed at particular times: around birth, before starting to learn the scriptures, at marriage and around death.

Different families have their own customs, but children are always present, except possibly at funeral ceremonies. They will join the celebrations for a baby brother or sister, niece or nephew, and be invited with the whole family to weddings of aunts and uncles, cousins and friends.

# What is caste?

*"From my point of view, there are lots of Hindus, but they are from different castes."*

Rites and relationships are not affected just by a person's family. Caste is important as well.

Varna

In ancient India, there were four main groups of people: brahmins, kshatriyas, vaishyas and shudras. The brahmins were originally priests, the kshatriyas kings and warriors. The vaishyas were merchants and the shudras the servants. These groups are called '**varnas**'. When people speak of 'caste', they sometimes mean 'varna'.

Varna affects things like festivals and samskaras. Some festivals were traditionally linked with one varna: Rakshabandhan for brahmins, Dassehra for kshatriyas, Divali for vaishyas and so on. Nowadays, though, people don't take too much notice of this and celebrate all together.

Varna does still affect the samskaras. For example, the sacred thread ceremony is meant to be performed only by members of the first three varnas. They are called '**dvija**' or 'twice-born'. In practice, it is mainly brahmins who keep up the ceremony. For them, it is very important. A brahmin boy must have been given his sacred thread before he gets married.

*Sacred thread ceremony*

Traditionally, a boy received his sacred thread and then went to live with a teacher for a while. He would start to learn the *Vedas*, the ancient scriptures which only dvijas were allowed to hear.

Nowadays, it's rather different. The boy goes back to school like everyone else after the celebrations. But the rites themselves remain the same. A priest makes special offerings into the **sacred fire**. He loops the white cotton cord over the boy's left shoulder and under his right arm. He teaches the boy the Gayatri Mantra (⟶ page 14), which stands for all the Vedas. Then the boy sets out, staff in hand, pretending to go to Kashi. Kashi is the great Indian city of learning and liberation, also called Banaras or Varanasi. With much hilarity, the boy's relatives catch him and carry him back to the hall where family and friends gather for a huge meal.

*A young brahmin in South India wearing the sacred thread.*

"It's very important to have your whole family around for the **upanayana** ceremony. My brother-in-law took his son to India when he was eleven, so they could celebrate with the family at Prayag, a very holy place for us. They're not religious, but the sacred thread is very important for brahmins. They always wear their sacred thread. When it wears out, you can buy a new one. Before you put it on, you have a bath and put some Ganges water on the new thread. It's all to do with purity — outside and inside yourself."

*Jati*

In everyday life, **jati** is much more important than varna. It is more accurate to use the word 'caste' to mean 'jati'. You are born into your jati. (It means 'birth'.) So you belong to the same jati as the rest of your family. Jatis used to be linked with traditional occupations: goldsmith caste, potter caste and so on. In Indian villages, your caste still affects where you live, whom you eat with, whom you marry and so on.

In Indian cities, many of these customs are dying out. But this doesn't mean that caste is no longer important to children growing up in Hinduism. They will know which caste they belong to and will be encouraged to marry someone from the same caste.

In big cities in Britain, many castes have special associations. These run social occasions, organise festivals, arrange satsangs and so on. They also raise money for charity and give assistance to caste members in need of help.

---

Each caste has certain surnames connected with it. Castes and names vary from region to region in India. Here are a few examples originating from *Gujarat* and **Uttar Pradesh**.

| CASTE | TRADITIONAL OCCUPATION | NAMES |
|-------|------------------------|-------|
| Mochi | Shoemaker | *Chudasama* |
| Bania | Business people | *Shah, Mehta,* ***Agrawal*** |
| Soni | Goldsmith | *Patni, Raniga* |
| Kumbha | Potter | *Varia, Ladwa* |
| Brahmin | Priest/scholar | *Joshi, Vyas,* ***Pandey, Misra, Shukla*** |

---

# Getting married

For many Hindus, caste is still very important when a marriage partner is being chosen. This is partly why marriages are 'arranged'. But it is not the only reason...

*"Whenever I go into schools and talk to pupils about being a Hindu, they always ask me about this. 'I wouldn't like to have an arranged marriage', they say.*

| wanted brides | wanted brides |
|---|---|
| A WELL EDUCATED BUSINESS CLASS AGRAWAL FAMILY INVITES PROPOSAL FOR THEIR SON 29/167 C.M., C.A., ICWA, M.B.A. (U.S.A.), M.S. (U.S.A.) SETTLED IN AMERICA SEEKS WELL EDUCATED GIRL OF REPUTED FAMILY. SEND FULL DETAIL IN 1ST INSTANCE. WRITE BOX G 165-D, TIMES OF INDIA, BOMBAY 400 001. | EZHUVA FAMILY WELL-SETTLED IN BOMBAY SEEKS ALLIANCE FOR THEIR SON, 29/188, MECHANICAL ENGINEER, EMPLOYED WITH HIGH SALARY, FROM PARENTS OF SMART EZHUVA GIRLS HAVING GOOD FAMILY BACKGROUND. WRITE WITH FULL DETAILS BOX A, 279-D, TIMES OF INDIA, BOMBAY 400 001. |

*Marriage ads similar to these have long pre-dated computer dating in the Indian Press.*

*It's partly what you're used to. We trust our parents to find someone suitable for us. If you marry someone from the same caste, it will be easier to get on with them and their family.*

*Lots of English people fall in love and get married and then they find they can't get on together, so they get divorced. If you marry someone you don't know, you take time. You learn how to get on together.*

*I hope my daughter will have an arranged marriage. Even though she is only ten, my husband tells her, 'We will find a nice Hindu boy for you'. She knows that this is what we hope for when she is older."*

In many ways, Hindu children are brought up to consider other people before themselves. Respect for elders is a duty which it is an honour to perform. So they may be prepared to see the benefits of having an arranged marriage. This doesn't mean, of course, that there are never any problems or that people always agree with their parents' choice.

*"When I was about 12, I used to worry that my parents would choose a boy from India and make me go and live there. I'd never been to India, so it would have been very strange. Actually, my fiancé has lived in England for most of his life. His family came from Kenya, like my mum and dad."*

*"My parents brought home this boy, but I didn't want to marry him! They say, 'When will you get married?' but I shall wait till I feel the time is right."*

*"I'm glad I've had an arranged marriage. My parents didn't bother with the horoscopes. They just tried to find someone they knew would make me happy."*

*"I can choose who I marry within our community. I went to a wedding the other day. There was a really good-looking young priest. I thought, 'He couldn't be my husband, he's so good-looking', but I'm still hoping! I'll send you an invitation . . ."*

# The wedding

*Wedding invitation*

Hindu wedding invitations, like the weddings themselves, are often lavish affairs. They show symbols of good luck for the marriage, including pictures of Ganesh, the god who removes obstacles.

Invitations include the whole family, so weddings are an opportunity for children as well as adults to put on their best clothes and enjoy the colourful ceremonies. Silk saris, gleaming with gold, rustle as the guests mingle in the marriage hall.

*Two young girls join the bride and bridegroom on the swing.*

## Wedding customs

Though customs vary greatly, the younger children are usually free to wander right up to the place where the bride and groom sit with their attendants and the priest. They may watch as the bride's sari is tied to a cloth around the groom's neck and listen as the couple's horoscopes are read out. When the guests pour forward to bring their presents, children will be there too.

Sometimes, children have a special role. At a South Indian brahmin wedding, two young nieces of the bride attended her. At a Gujarati wedding in Northwest London, two small boys proudly carried in a deep green cloth. The bride and groom stood together behind the cloth to make their offerings of rice and ghee to the sacred fire.

Then they took seven steps together. As Hindu couples have done through the ages, they prayed that their marriage would be blessed by children.

The groom says to the bride:

Take the first step for strength.
Take the second step for power.
Take the third step for prosperity.
Take the fourth step for happiness.
Take the fifth step for children.
Take the sixth step for enjoyment of pleasures.
Take the seventh step for close union.
May God be your guide.
May we be blessed with children.

Having taken seven steps with me, become my friend.
With utmost love to each other...may we walk together.
May we make our minds united.
I am the melody, you are the words.
You are the melody, I am the words.

*Bride and groom in front of the sacred fire.*

# A child is born

## "May we be blessed with children"

Ceremonies for a baby's well-being start even before it is born. Different families have different customs, but some important times are: the seventh (or ninth) month of a first pregnancy, the birth, six days after the birth (for Gujaratis), the baby's first outing, the first haircut and so on. Often there is a special part for children to play, as in this Gujarati version of the seemantham ceremony:

*"When you are expecting your first baby, there is a ceremony to say, 'Welcome to parenthood'. Because we worship Ambama, we make a shrine for her and invite some little girls for a meal. Relatives on both sides come.*

*The parents of the mother-to-be bring a red or green cloth with some special things tied up in it — coconut, betel nut, mung beans. It is held by a woman who has a child already but has never had a miscarriage. She passes it back and forward seven times to the mother-to-be. It shows their concern that the baby will be safely born.*

*Children pick up the special meanings of many of the customs. Something sweet on the baby's tongue to hope it will be sweet! Pen and paper for the goddess Vidatha — the baby's future is her concern. Coconuts and mung beans for good luck, like the* **swastika** *sign. Red and green — auspicious colours, encouraging what is good."*

*First outing*

*"It's a tradition not to go out for five weeks. This time I had to go out for one or two things, but I didn't take the baby. On its first outing, the baby is taken to a religious place like a temple. But before it goes, the priest blesses the baby.*

*A friend of my father-in-law lives in Leicester. We look up to him, because he is so devoted to our goddess, Amba. He has a large shrine in his house. We have taken all three girls there for their first outing. One of our English friends was surprised. She thought 75 miles to Leicester was a long way to go. But I wouldn't have minded travelling even more than that, because it has a religious meaning for us."*
(Gujarati mother)

## First haircut

*"This may be done age one or three. You shave the child's hair off. It shouldn't just be thrown away. You put it into flowing water, if possible, the River Ganges. In India, my family lived near the Jumna River, which is also holy, so we used to go there.*

*In this country, I didn't want to shave the whole of my daughter's head. So when she was one, I just cut her hair and wrapped up what I had cut off. Then when she was fourteen months, I took it to the Ganges."*
(Brahmin mother from Uttar Pradesh)

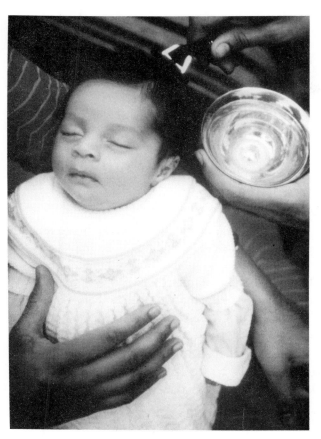

*A Hindu child's first haircut.*

The hair, symbolising 'the burden of birth', is carried away. The parents hope that the child will not suffer in this life for anything bad done in a previous life (→ page 59). Though they will not understand this yet, even quite young children can tell you what is done:

*"I can remember when my sister had her hair shaved. We put her in the high chair and the barber came. We put her hair in the river. When I was little, I used to cry when I watched the video of me, because I cried when he shaved my head."* (Girl aged 5)

It's very common to have videos of special occasions now: first haircut, sacred thread ceremony, marriage and so on. Watching videos of other people is a good way of learning what happens at such times. And children can enjoy watching themselves perform before they became camera-shy!

# Growing up

*"My children are used to thinking about God. They see me saying prayers every day. If we have a statue of Krishna in our home, we have to treat it properly. So each morning I say the prayers to wake the god up and at night the girls put him to bed. It's a rush in the morning to have a bath and offer the god food, but they know it's important.*

*The other day, I had to go away for the night. When I came back, my five year old said, 'Guess what, Mummy?'*
*'You forgot to feed the god?'*
*'No, we didn't!'*
*She and my husband had said the prayers. I felt so proud of her."*

Although many Hindu families are not as religious as this, children are often encouraged to take responsibility for themselves and others. The five ancient daily duties or sacrifices are: to meditate, make offerings to the gods, honour your elders, be hospitable to guests, care for all living things. Hospitality, respect and consideration are likely to be highly valued, however small a part 'religion' plays in a family's day to day affairs.

*Fasting*

Fasting is another practice which is common even in families who say they're not religious. As at some festivals, fasting does not usually mean going without food altogether. There are all kinds of fasts: weekly, fortnightly, monthly, annual, or for some particular purpose.

*"On the eleventh day each fortnight — we call it Agyaras — we don't have turmeric or flour. You must try to have potatoes with salt and black pepper. It's a sort of tradition. Then there's a fast for five days when you go without salt for finding a husband. But I didn't do it. It didn't seem important."*

For some Hindus, fasting is just a tradition which they sometimes keep. For others, it has a deeper meaning.

*"We fast every Tuesday, because it is the day of goddess Ambama. It's to help you spiritually. You can have fruit, tea, coffee, milk, juices. We are allowed just one meal. But no grains.*

*Today, people have everything — nice houses, big cars — everything except peace of mind. Strict fasting gives you that. You feel happy inside and closer to God. It even makes a difference to my five year old. She pays more attention when she knows her mother and father are fasting. She asks, 'Mummy, are you all right? Do you want me to get you anything?'"*

---

Work out a day's menu for a busy mother who is keeping a weekly fast day. Remember that the children will need feeding normally.
Her single meal will need to be nutritious — but no meat, eggs, or cereals.

Use the information above and an Indian cookery book, if possible.

---

*Guests at a Hindu house-warming party.*

# What happens when we die?

While children are encouraged to take a full part in birth, sacred thread and marriage ceremonies, it is not usual for them to go to funerals.

*"It is a sad time and we don't want the children to be sad. I remember when we were in India, my aunt died. We were all sent to another aunt's until the funeral was over."*

Outside India, funerals normally take place at a crematorium. In India, it is usual for the body to be cremated on a funeral pyre beside a river. The eldest son or close male relative lights the pyre, while the priest says special Sanskrit mantras. Later, the ashes will be taken to the river, the Ganges, if possible, and sprinkled in its purifying waters. Hindus living abroad will often take the ashes back to an Indian river, when they have a chance.

After India's Prime Minister, Mrs Gandhi, was assassinated, pictures of her funeral were shown on television around the world.

*"It gave me a chance to explain to the children what happens. I pointed out the way the sandalwood was piled up and how pure clarified butter was used to keep the fire burning. I taught them a verse from the Ramayan, which is said by the priest, 'The body is made up of the five elements: earth, water, fire, air and sky'."*

Another very well-known verse said at funerals comes from the Gita:

**"The soul is not killed when the body is slain."**

The idea is that the body returns to the elements, but the soul or real self of the person lives on. That soul or **atman** will then be reborn in another body, according to the good or bad deeds done in that and other previous lives. This belief in rebirth is sometimes called reincarnation, or, a bit inaccurately, karma. 'Karma' means 'action', so it refers to the idea that what we do (how we act) in this life has consequences for future lives.

*"This is a difficult idea. We wouldn't usually teach it to children till they were about twelve or thirteen — when they had lived a little, so they have some experience of life. Otherwise, they won't understand it."*

But this does not mean that quite young children, like those of other religions, do not have questions to ask about dying.

*"My little daughter thinks a lot about God. She woke up in the middle of the night recently and asked me, 'Mummy, what happens when we die?' I told her that we go to be with God. She asked if we would not die if we said our prayers, but I told her that everyone has to die. Her next question was, 'If I pray a lot, will I go quickly?' I said that we have to stay here and do good things first.*

*Then she asked me what it was like when we die. I had to tell her that nobody knows that, but we would be with God."*

At first sight, this seems a strange answer. It doesn't seem to have anything to do with rebirth. Is it just the sort of thing parents tell their children to keep them quiet?

Actually, it is a very Hindu answer. Indian teachers have always realised that there is no point in teaching a person something he or she can't possibly understand at the moment. Instead, give pupils something they can grasp. Then later, they will be able to see deeper meanings in what they have been taught.

'Doing good things' is something familiar to the little girl already. Later she will see how it fits in with the hope of achieving a better rebirth.

'Being with God' also has meaning for her, as the family prays morning and night. And for Hindus, the aim is *not* to go on being reborn for ever, but to be free from the cycle of rebirth. People have different beliefs about this **moksha** or liberation. But for many it is thought of as the blissful union of the atman with God for ever.

# Special journeys

There are many reasons why Hindus living abroad might want to visit India: to see relatives, to perform certain ceremonies, to go to holy places or just to find out what it is like if you've never lived there yourself.

> Make an illustrated timechart of a Hindu's life, showing the different occasions when a visit to India might be thought important.

*Pilgrimages*

It's a tradition for Hindus in old age to go on pilgrimage round India 'to see the places of God'. They may travel thousands of miles to bathe in the real River Ganges, to visit Rameshvaram in the South or Dvarka, Krishna's capital city in the West.

Badrinath high in the Himalayas is famous as a place of renunciation. Here, people turn their backs on material possessions. In caves, on mountains, holy men live simple lives, seeking for truth and liberation. Not all visitors are that high-minded, though.

*"Lots of people go as sightseers to escape from the heat of the cities. The views up there are marvellous. Just near the temple at Badrinath is the warm spring near the source of the Ganges. The air's very cold and crisp, but you always bathe before doing puja in the temple. It purifies you − a sign of taking away your sins.*

*My mother wanted to go on a pilgrimage there, so my sister took her, and her three young children went too. They were so excited. When they got up there, my mother wanted the little one to bathe. My sister said, 'No, he's too young. He'll catch cold!' But my mother just dumped him in the spring!*

*I have been to Badrinath as a sightseer and made all the offerings. When my husband retires, we hope to go back together as pilgrims."*

From the beginning of their lives, Hindu children are immersed in the cultural traditions of their religion. Through food and dress, language and family relationships, their lives will be influenced by their Hindu upbringing. Their reactions to the traditional stories, customs and beliefs will, of course, vary. Some will always remain uninvolved − like the Badrinath tourist, enjoying the view, perhaps, but not bothering about anything else. Others will be like those travellers who make offerings at the temple — glad to feel at home with such religious traditions. Still others will return as pilgrims — looking to the stories and beliefs for deeper meanings. They will seek truth and happiness in the ever richer patterns which they first learnt when growing up in Hinduism.

*Hindu pilgrims gather at the source of the Ganges.*

# Glossary

**ārti**  offering of lights

**ātman**  soul, true self

**bhajan**  devotional song

**Bráhman**  Supreme Reality, True God

**brāhmin**  priest, member of first varna

**burfi**  milk sweet

**dandya**  stick used in Navratri dance

**darshan**  'seeing'; realising God's presence

**dīvā**  lamp

**dvija**  'twice-born'; member of first three varnas

**Gáyatrī Mantra**  very important verse from Vedas; said each day, especially by brahmins

**ghee**  clarified butter

**gopī**  milkmaid; one of Krishna's beloved companions

**gulab jamon**  milk sweet in syrup

**ishtadeva**  chosen god, own preferred form of God

**ISKCON**  International Society for Krishna Consciousness (Hare Krishna Movement)

**jalebi**  sweet batter in syrup

**jāti**  'birth'; caste

**jay jay**  'Victory'; a greeting to gods

**kīrtan**  session for singing bhajans

**ladoo**  sweet

**linga/ling**  black stone; form in which Shiva is worshipped

**mandir**  temple; shrine

**mantra**  sacred verse, usually in Sanskrit

**moksha**  liberation; freedom from rebirth

**mūrti**  image (statue) of god/goddess

**prashād**  (food) blessed by being offered to gods

**pūjā**  worship; offerings

**rangoli (chauk, álpana)**  pattern made to welcome god

**rupee**  unit of modern Indian currency

**sacred fire**  lit at marriage and other ceremonies; represents Agni, god of fire, God as witness

**samskāra**  purifying ceremony, e.g. at birth, death, etc.

**Sanskrit**  'perfect' language of the ancient scriptures

**satsang**  gathering for devotional singing/ worship

**swāmi**  respected leader or teacher

**Swāminārāyan Movement**  modern Hindu movement strong among Gujaratis

**swastika**  ancient Indian symbol of good fortune

**upanáyana**  sacred thread ceremony

**varna**  one of four groups in traditional Hindu society: brahmins, kshatriyas, vaishyas, shudras (priests, princes and warriors, merchants, service craftsmen)

# A guide to pronunciation

The following guide will help you in the pronunciation of words:

Short 'a' as in 'but'
Long 'a' as in 'part'
'e' as in 'bay'
Long 'i' as in 'beet'
'o' as in 'boat'
Long 'u' as in 'pool'

'h' is pronounced separately except after 's'.

In the glossary long vowels have a line above them. An acute sign ( ' ) shows which syllable to stress.

# Index

# Acknowledgements

I would like to express my very grateful thanks to the following, who helped by sharing their experiences of growing up in Hinduism. Without them this book would not have been possible:

Vijju Churchman, Daksa Dattani, Tina Shah and family, G.N. Vachhani and family, Valbai Vellani, Rita Vyas, S. Rajalakshmi Rajan and family.

I am especially grateful to Geeta Pandey, who acted as consultant for this book, and her daughter Shivani.

We are grateful to the following for permission to reproduce photographs and other copyright material;

Argus Communications, B. Kapur/Shostal Associates, *Religion in Human Culture, the Hindu Tradition*, page 39; Edward Arnold, Damodar Sharma, *Hindu Belief and Practice*, page 14; John Hillelson Agency/Raghubir Singh, page 61; Jean Holm, page 31; India Book House Educational Trust, Amar Chitra Katha, *Shiva Parvati*, page 11; courtesy ISKCON, pages 22, 28 and 29; Bob Jackson, page 33; Ann and Bury Peerless Slide Resources and Picture Library, pages 19, 34 and 49; Picturepoint, page 24; Popperfoto, page 58; Sauresh Ray, pages 27, 30 and 56; David Richardson, page 44; David Rose, page 35; Sacred Trinity Centre, page 55; courtesy Shree Sanatan Mandir, Leicester, pages 20 and 36 above; Slide Centre, Ilminster, page 53; Sree Kalaimagal Industries, pages 13 and 15; courtesy Swami Narayan Temple, London, page 40; John Walmsley, page 17. Pages 20, 22, 28, 29, 36 above and 37 by Jacqueline Hirst.

Cover: Candles being lit during Divali festival. Hutchison Library (photo: Liba Taylor)

LONGMAN GROUP UK LIMITED
*Longman House, Burnt Mill, Harlow, Essex, CM20 2JE, England
and Associated Companies throughout the World.*

First published 1990
ISBN 0 582 00285 0

Produced by Longman Group (FE) Ltd
Printed in Hong Kong